Pyramids

BY NANCY FURSTINGER

Published by The Child's World®
1980 Lookout Drive • Mankato, MN 56003-1705
800-599-READ • www.childsworld.com

Acknowledgments
The Child's World®: Mary Berendes, Publishing Director
Red Line Editorial: Editorial direction
The Design Lab: Design

Photographs ©: Kokhanchikov/Shutterstock Images,
cover (bottom left), 1 (bottom left), 10; Dennis Steen/
Shutterstock Images, cover (top left), 1 (top left), 3 (left);
Kheng Guan Toh/Shutterstock Images, cover (bottom
right), 1 (bottom right), 9; Plus Lee/Shutterstock Images,
cover (top right), 1 (top right), 3 (right), 12; Remi
Cauzid/Shutterstock Images, 4; Shutterstock Images,
5, 6, 14, 21; Sanchai Khudpin/Shutterstock Images,
11; Z. H. Chen/Shutterstock Images, 15; M. Bonotto/
Shutterstock Images, 17; Frank L Junior/Shutterstock
Images, 18; Craig Wactor/Shutterstock Images, 22

ISBN 9781623239855
LCCN 2013947244

Printed in the United States of America
Mankato, MN
November, 2013
PA02194

ABOUT THE AUTHOR

Award-winning author Nancy
Furstinger enjoys searching
for inspiring shapes in nature
as she hikes with her big
pooches. She is the author of
more than 100 books.

CONTENTS

AT THE FARMERS' MARKET

Sellers at the market stack their fruit in pyramids, too!

You've helped your mother make yummy blackberry jam. Now it's time to sell jars of jam to hungry customers at the farmers' market. Stack the jars so they look nice. Each level of jars is smaller than the levels below it. Crown the top with the final jar.

The booth next door sells handmade toys. You pick up cloth juggling bags and toss them around. Did you notice the shape of the juggling bags is like the shape of the jam jar stack? Both of these shapes are **pyramids**.

Are any of your toys shaped like pyramids?

WHAT DOES A PYRAMID LOOK LIKE?

Pyramids are all around us. Pyramids have three **dimensions**. These shapes are not flat. Flat shapes, like triangles, have only two dimensions: length and width. These flat shapes are also called plane shapes or 2-D shapes.

Shapes that have three dimensions like pyramids are **3-D** shapes. A pyramid's three dimensions are length, width, and height. We can measure all three dimensions. 3-D shapes are also called solid shapes.

How can we identify a pyramid? Look closely. A pyramid has a flat bottom, called a **base**. Many pyramids have a square base. Some pyramids have a triangle base. A pyramid's base can even have five, six, or more sides.

Matching triangles form the sides of a pyramid. Each triangle is one of the pyramid's **faces**. These faces are two-dimensional flat **surfaces**. Each face forms a surface of a 3-D shape. The faces come to a point at the top. The point is called a **vertex**. The place where any two faces meet is called an **edge**.

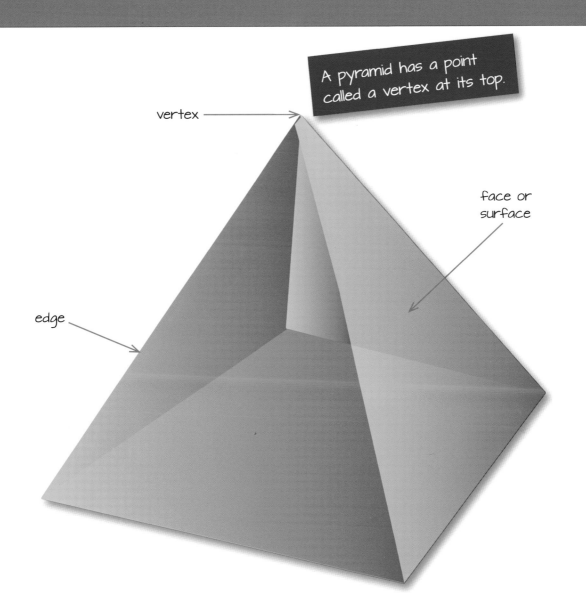

A pyramid has a point called a vertex at its top.

vertex

face or surface

edge

PLAYING IN PYRAMIDS

Once you know what a pyramid looks like, you'll spot this 3-D shape all around. You'll start seeing pyramids in everyday objects.

At the library, there's a special tent with a pointy top. Inside, cozy pillows and a stack of books greet readers. Your family has a tent almost the same shape. It has a square

bottom with four sides sloping up. You slept in the tent when you went camping.

After reading, it's time to burn off energy on the playground. Climb up the jungle gym. Who will reach the pointy top first?

Can you spot the pyramids at this playground?

THE GREAT PYRAMIDS

The world's most famous pyramids are in Egypt. Three pyramids rise above Giza, near the city of Cairo. The pyramids have lasted more than 4,500 years.

The largest, the Great Pyramid, once stood 481 feet (147 m) tall. That is nearly as high as a 50-story building. Today it is shorter.

The Pyramids of Giza, Egypt, have stood for thousands of years.

Some stones at the top fell off or were removed.

Pyramids were built to honor the Egyptian pharaohs, or kings. Inside the pyramids were placed the kings' tombs. After death, the kings' bodies were preserved and wrapped in cloth. These mummies were buried with many things to help the kings live in the next world. When scientists unearthed tombs, they discovered jewelry, tools, food, toys, servants, and pets.

An Ancient Mystery

Some secrets about the Great Pyramid remain to this day. Thousands of workers cut, moved, and then fit together more than 2 million stone blocks. Some blocks weighed as much as two elephants! How did the workers haul these blocks? Scientists today aren't sure, but they believe it only took a few decades.

PYRAMID BUILDINGS

The pyramid shape has inspired modern-day builders. A glass and steel pyramid greets museum visitors in Paris, France. Three smaller pyramids border the big one at the Louvre museum.

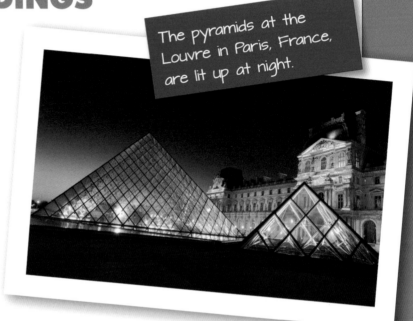

The Pyramids at the Louvre in Paris, France, are lit up at night.

A stainless steel pyramid in Memphis, Tennessee, rises above the Mississippi River. The Pyramid Arena is the third-largest pyramid in the world.

Skyscraper Pyramid

Skyscrapers tower above San Francisco. The Transamerica building is the tallest skyscraper in the city. The concrete, glass, and steel building has a wide base. This helps it withstand earthquakes. At first, the builder designed a much taller pyramid. However, people worried this would ruin their view of the San Francisco Bay.

The Transamerica building casts a smaller shadow than a regular building would. This lets more light down to the streets below.

15

FLYING PYRAMIDS

A breezy day is perfect for flying your new kite!
You made the kite using fishing lines, drinking
straws, and tissue paper. Its pyramid shape helps
your kite soar.

A famous inventor once made a similar kite.
More than 100 years ago, Alexander Graham Bell
wanted to create a flying machine. He used a strong
frame for his kite. He named it *Cygnet*. It was a big
pyramid made of nearly 3,400 smaller pyramids!
The kite carried a pilot in the flight seat. Cygnet flew
for seven minutes.

This pyramid kite has a base shaped like a triangle.

17

It's fun to build pyramids in the sand!

PYRAMIDS IN THE SAND

The beach is a lot of fun on a summer day. Today, there is a sand castle competition going on. Someone has built a copy of an Egyptian pyramid. In front of the pyramid is the Sphinx. The Sphinx has the body of a lion and the head of a person. People from ancient Greece and Egypt told stories about the Sphinx.

Build your own sand pyramid. Then if you get hot, go under a beach umbrella. The umbrella is shaped like a pyramid, too!

PYRAMIDS IN NATURE

You can find pyramid shapes in nature. Some mountain peaks form this shape. Pyramid Peak in California looks like a huge granite pyramid. Mount Rtanj in Serbia has the same shape. Some people believe aliens created this peak thousands of years ago! But scientists don't think that is true.

Landforms called plugs form when molten rock from volcanoes hardens. Two of these plugs, the Pitons, are on the island of Saint Lucia. The twin pyramid-shaped peaks rise above the Caribbean waters.

Search for pyramid shapes in your house or out and about. You'll be amazed how many of these 3-D shapes you can discover all around you!

The Matterhorn in Switzerland is a famous pyramid-shaped peak.

HANDS-ON ACTIVITY: PENNY PYRAMID

Save up your spare pennies to make this model of a pyramid. Then display your shiny 3-D shape in a special spot!

Materials

- pennies
- shallow dish
- salt
- lemon juice
- glue
- pyramid-shaped Styrofoam piece

Directions

1. First, make your pennies sparkle. Place them in the dish. Add a teaspoon of salt and pour in lemon juice until it covers the pennies. Wait a few minutes, then rinse and dry.
2. Once your pennies are dry, glue them to the pyramid shape. Start at the top. Glue one penny to each side.
3. Keep adding an additional penny to each lower row.
4. Display your pyramid so everyone can admire it!

GLOSSARY

base (BASE): A base is a flat surface on a 3-D shape. A pyramid's base can have three, four, or more sides.

dimensions (duh-MEN-shuns): Dimensions are the length, width, or height of an object. A pyramid's height is one of its dimensions.

edge (EJ): An edge is the line where a surface begins or ends. A pyramid's edge is where the base meets the pyramid's sides.

faces (FASE-uhs): Faces are flat surfaces on a 3-D shape. A pyramid has several faces.

pyramids (PIR-uh-mids): Pyramids are 3-D shapes with a base with three, four, or more sides that meet at the top in a point. The sides of pyramids are triangles.

surfaces (SUR-fas-uhs): Surfaces are the flat or curved borders of a 3-D shape. A pyramid has several flat surfaces.

3-D (THREE-DEE): A 3-D shape has three dimensions, length, width, and height. A 3-D shape is not flat.

vertex (VUR-teks): A vertex is the point where the edges of a 3-D shape meet. A pyramid has one vertex at its point.

BOOKS

Anderson, Moira. *Shapes in Our World.* Huntington Beach, CA: Teacher Created Materials Publishing, 2009.

Cohen, Marina. *My Path to Math: 3-D Shapes.* New York: Crabtree Publishing Company, 2011.

WEB SITES

Visit our Web site for links about Pyramids: *childsworld.com/links*

Note to Parents, Teachers, and Librarians:
We routinely verify our Web links to make sure they are safe and active sites. So encourage your readers to check them out!

INDEX